Possum, Beaver, Lion: Variants

poems by

Sarah Voss

Finishing Line Press
Georgetown, Kentucky

Possum, Beaver, Lion: Variants

For Sonna, Wil, Melinda, Dan and all the rest of our incredible family, for the members of my long-time writing group Cheryl, Gladys, Lorraine, Pat; and for all the others who have helped me with my poetry in both big and small ways.

A special note of appreciation for cover artist Raya Lehan and the beautiful cover she produced.

Copyright © 2017 by Sarah Voss
ISBN 978-1-63534-311-3 First Edition
All rights reserved under International and Pan-American Copyright Conventions.
No part of this book may be reproduced in any manner whatsoever without written permission from the publisher, except in the case of brief quotations embodied in critical articles and reviews.

ACKNOWLEDGMENTS

On the Eve of a Hard Seventy was a finalist in the 2015 Princemere Poetry Prize.

Thirteen and Sixty-nine received honorable mention in the Poetry Across the Generations Contest, Sigma Phi Omega, Omaha UNO, 2014.

Haven was first published in *Celebrate: A Collection of Women's Writings (XVI)* Omaha: UNO, 2012.

Publisher: Leah Maines

Editor: Christen Kincaid

Cover Art: Raya Lehan

Author Photo: Matt Goodlett

Cover Design: Raya Lehan

Printed in the USA on acid-free paper.
Order online: www.finishinglinepress.com
        also available on amazon.com

                Author inquiries and mail orders:
                     Finishing Line Press
                       P. O. Box 1626
                Georgetown, Kentucky 40324
                         U. S. A.

Table of Contents

Some Suggest 1

Possum 2
Dangling Modifier 3
Old-Fashioned Treasure Hunt 4
The Widower 7
Thirteen 8
Sixty-nine 9
The Weed that Turned into a Zinnia 10
Evasion 11
Accident 12

Beaver 13
Adding a Room 14
The Stories You've Taught Me 15
Fears Flying 17
The People Who Lived Here Before: A Response 18
The Pictures Are Back on the Walls 21
Lady Jekyll's Story 22
Snow Crab Apple Tree 23

Lion 24
How You Know I'm Mad: A Response to your "Poem in
  7 Parts" 25
I Am the Plumber's Wife 27
On the Eve of a Hard Seventy 28
The Mail Arrives Late 30
Things My Husband Doesn't Know I Do 31
Haven 32
Another Breadstick Please 33
May Day 35

Some Suggest

we deceive the gods, pretend
blindness lest they take
unwelcome notice of us
and foul our dreams. Possum.

Some say we should pray
every day for an hour. When
we are really busy we should
pray for two hours. Beaver.

I suggest we rage and roar
when our dreams are broken,
help the gods see how we hope
to imitate their bravery. Lion.

Possum: act a part, affect, alternative reality, assume, badger, blindness, coquet, counterfeit, deceive, deception, dissemble, dissimulate, don't look, double presentation, feign, fool, glutton, good show, hide, hidden, ignore, illusion, limited sight, limited vision, malinger, pass off for, play dumb, play false, pretend, puzzle, put on, sham, simulate, trickery, two world views.

Dangling Modifier

Forty years ago when I was in a gap
in my life, I decided to write stories.
In hindsight, I see I had potential, but
what I wanted was success, not possibility,
so when by God's grace an able old gent
two houses away offered to help prune
my craft, my pride was too large for me
to see past the red ink scribbles he
plastered so caringly all over my pages.
I hope I recall correctly when I say
I did manage to thank him, though I still
regret the absence of sweet in my response

which comes back to me now after
a young colleague reprimanded me
for interfering in his work, my intentions
being anything but.

                                        illusion

The Old-Fashioned Treasure Hunt

Right off, Gretchen knew, her 10-year-old brain fresh, active,
no speck of cognitive despair like mine, 7 times older. Plus, her search:
an alternative reality, though surely we shared the same sweet space.

> *Clue 1. 1014 100 2125*
> *Look down and all around.*

"Mindcraft?" she whispered shyly.

"What?" I replied, dumb as any grandparent could be, but already
her tiny hands plied her computer, which promptly paid out

> *Clue 2. Under the reading by the throne, all alone.*

I prayed for insight, fast and accurate, hoping to occult my ignorance.
Neither of us could offer much, but we were saved by the bell,
no, not a bell from my 60-years-ago youth,
but a computer bell-squeal which, right off, Gretchen knew

was her parents Skyping from vacation-land. "A toilet can be a throne,"
she told them. Her voice, a complete puzzle. "I'm stuck," she said.

"Sleep on it," Papa replied. His Skyped smile swept the screen.

I related to the toilet throne. "Did you check under the bathroom
basket?" Jackpot! Dusty, maybe, but my brain still worked.

> *Clue 3: In the 7th letter's museum...*

Stumped. Me more than she.

Another day, another Skype. Somehow she knew
that the "7th letter" (a,b,c,d,e,f,G) meant "Gretchen" **(of course)**
and "museum" meant "art gallery" and until then I'd barely glanced
at the schooled artwork taped across the hall wall,
yet there, slipped behind the picture she'd drawn of **home**, hid

> *Clue 4. Sorry, Mom. Hi Gretchen,*
> *Welcome back, Papa. If you like to whirl*
> *give me a spin.*

My brain let out a kind of pathetic cry,
but I forced a nonchalant shoulder shrug.

G-daughter grinned. "X Box," she guessed.

"What?" I replied, still dumb as any grandparent could be.

"That's what the X Box says," she said, but I didn't really understand
until the next night when we were watching *Willy Wonka
and the Chocolate Factory*. My beloved little relative,
already a few inches taller than the last visit, faced the TV.

"X Box on," she commanded and the screen lit up:
Sorry Mom. Hi, Gretchen. Welcome back, Papa.

"Movie, play," she authorized, and it did.

> *Clue 5. Hard, easy, or scrambled inside...*

Two days earlier, right after Clue 1, Gretchen already knew.
We were making sugar cookies for the school bake sale the next day.
"G" pulled up her favorite recipe on her ipad
and we creamed the sugar, the butter, the two eggs.

"What's this?" I asked holding up one of the two remaining eggs
in the carton. "It's been blown out."

"Oh," G said, "Papa blew it out. There's a piece of paper
rolled up inside. It must be the prize."

"Gretchen, think," I wished. And she did.
"We shouldn't look," she said. "He'd be disappointed."

My granddaughter, the brain-genius.

So we didn't look until after we'd found all the clues,
and after Gretchen cracked the egg shell while we were Skyping
and after she read the note that said she and one friend
would get a 2-day trip to the inside water slide
and her eyes danced just like any kid's would have 60 years ago
and her parents looked like the world was perfect
and I, just as smart as any grandparent, uttered not one

word about the set of answers my foresighted son left
under the table by the bed "just in case"
my brilliant young granddaughter might need extra help.

puzzle

The Widower

Two daughters spoke at the ceremony.
Two grandchildren read Biblical passages.
Another shared a poem, then the oldest,
fifteen, told "ten things we all loved
about Grandma"—her cookies,

her art lessons... how she loved them all.
Earlier, the widower addressed the mourners,
—a substantial turnout, really, for someone
who'd moved so recently (closer to her girls)
and even then both she and the new widower

had known the odds, though they'd hidden
them like a cat secreting kittens, thinking
this simple act would protect their young kin,
a noble goal (regardless the cost).
So the widower, surrounded by those

he loved, sheltered by love
returned, stoic in his commentary,
a brave man paying tribute
to the woman he adored and the life
fully-lived, though far too short and thus

he set the public standard for visible tears.
From the corner of my own too-wet eye, I,
the widower's sister, couldn't help noticing
his wife's late mother and my own late
mother (my brother's mother)

standing slightly to the left of the poignant new
portrait of my brother's beloved and rather too
close to the mostly invisible church organist,
in spite of harboring a sure sense of welcome
and comfort, both of them were weeping profusely.

                                              hiding

Thirteen

Her emotions ride inside
on a teeter-totter. Up. Down.
Glad. Sad. Twenty. Six.

She studies hard. Then refuses to.
She plays piano like a pro. Then
breaks into tears when I applaud.
She paints my old mail box
to resemble a happy barn, then paints
her arms, her hands, her toes,
not noticing the prints she stamps
on the floor, the sink, the good
towel, yet she's so quick to change
when she finally sees the mess.

Good-natured. Sour. Bitter. Sweet.
She remembers everything
and when I haven't seen her
for a month or two, she's so much
bigger and even more beautiful
than she ever thought possible.

                                                            double presentation

Sixty-nine

My emotions ride inside
on escalators. Sometimes
I still take the stairs.
Up. Down. Glad. Sad.
Eighty-nine. Forty-nine.

I am wise but refuse
to tweet, blog, text, friend or
unfriend and I can't remember
the simplest new instructions.
I paint the old woodwork
just one more time, then fall
asleep at eight watching
my favorite show. I'm fun,
then grouchy. Edgy, then I listen
intently to everything my grandchild
says. When she slips and falls, I'm
first to find the right bandage,
call the doc, tell her it will all be fine.

When the time between visits grows
long, she's touched by how I've slowed
down and how much more she loves me
than I ever thought possible.

double reality

The Weed that Turned into a Zinnia

I spent forty years in the wilderness
one year selling one house, buying another.
More accurately I bought one house then,
months later, sold the first. Depression.
Despair. Uncertainty. Struggle.

In the spring, at the new house, after
the buying and before the selling,
along a row of well-established peonies,
I planted cosmos, zinnias, poppy seeds,
nasturtiums. When summer arrived
I saw I'd planted them too close
to those seasoned old perennials. Not

enough light everything needed every
thing was hard. I was tired. I worked best
I could, but my faith... a diamond lost.
A few flowers appeared anyway

in the pretense of a row. Cosmos maybe?
I transplanted them here and there,
watered them, loved them as they grew.
And grew. But no flowers. My spouse
wondered why I'd planted weeds in pots.

After the stalks grew stiff and huge,
I got rid of them, plucked God right out
of the dirt, tossed all sense of sacred
away. I fought with my spouse, finally
admitted wrong, pitched
those blasted weeds into the yard waste.

Early autumn I spotted a lone zinnia
blooming under the withering peonies.
I left it alone, took only
the joy of survival, which I stuck deep
in my heart, hoping.

feign

Evasion
    for Judy

My spouse disappears
behind a full-length mirror
leaving clear a spring view
from the side window.
The bottom fourth of a huge
scotch pine shows in reflection,
worn plastic flopping wildly
in the silent wind, a stray piece
of weed-proofing stuck amidst
aged bricks circling the ample
old tree-base like wagons
securing families around
campfire in an era now gone.

Not to worry, it's just my view
from the kitchen table as he
re-shelves the chocolate syrup
in the cupboard whose mirrored
back faces my chair—a mere
illusion, yet also a reality
in our relationship that happens
over and over as though this one
isn't enough anymore.

On the table, the red and pink
striated roses that he brought
yesterday and placed in fresh
water doctored with fine white
granules of floral preservative
will disappear that delicate bloom
within a week even though
I clip the stems hopefully
every single day.

                                            limited vision

Accident

Nasty, fault mine.
Idled left turning lane
Waiting break
Three lanes oncoming
Traffic rushing.
Similar tide rising

Tsunami.
Certain cars politely
Stopped.
Closest lane stopped.
Middle lane stopped.
Last lane beyond sight.

Never saw
speeding SUV
Third lane
Hit. Sentience lost.
Woke: thought
Hyundai burning

Wrong again: airbag
Forever deployed.
Right tire stuck
Construction hole.
No thing human broken.
Bruises.

Head injury.
Hearing loss.
Hard know
What friends mouth.

Conjunctions, prepositions
Other connections
Gone.

                                        trickery

Beaver: ambitious person, ball of fire, busy, begin again, builder, busy bee, busy person, doer, double effort, dynamo, eager, endless search, fireball, go-getter, hot shot, industrious, live wire, no slouch, more and more, over and over, pistol, re-blooms, self-starter, sharpy, sorcerer, spark plug, twice the work, workhorse.

Adding a Room[1]

Supposedly we're downsizing,
not building anew, but now I read
how longevity's extra 30 years
is a room added on, a room partly
determined by our present house,
partly shaped by our current needs,
yet an entity which unceasingly
demands unambiguous answers:
what new purpose will this room
meet? what meaning will it have?
how will it affect the air exchange
the heat, the echo of sounds,
even the traffic pattern
in the original house,

                              the bigness
and depth of which is why we
put the house on the market
in the first place, plus
all those stairs, and downsizing
seemed like a smart front door
rather than a bonus baby left
in a basket, needing
constant attention and nurture.

                                    builder

[1]with appreciation for Mary Catherine Bateson's metaphor in *Composing a Further Life*

The Stories You've Taught Me

Born nine months after
the coldest winter on record
in Dismal Seepage, Iowa,
your parents both beyond fifty
your father already Parkinsoned,
your siblings old enough
to be your parents but so proud
of you they were, you-little-angel
-you-devil, but, yes, definitely
more angel than devil
just ask Sr. Claire who never lied
nor you who just keep reiterating
all these marvelous stories

catching your audience unaware
over and over
through three wives and more lives
lies not ever quite lies
just embellished stories that wander
and entertain
and glisten with invention,
catching my heart unaware
over and over

until even I who never remember
jokes or tall tales or not so tall tales
even I know these stories,
can recite them by heart
as though they were mine to tell
over and over

all these marvelous stories
none of which I swear
are really why I love you
yet without which my love
would be untempered
like chocolate that turns out

flat and tacky for lack of stirring
over and over

                                                    over and over

Fears Flying

Only a handful
believe the impossible
is possible, only a few
of these few demonstrate
that the unachievable
can be achieved. They brush
our wings, groom
our engines, say yes
or tomorrow we'll try again
or we can still find a way
or I will help you. Then

they tease the feathers
we didn't even know we had
until we tickle the sky
with new-found hope, drop
seedlings from above
just as though we never doubted.

                                                industrious

The People Who Lived Here Before: A Response

0.
In imitation of, protest to, appreciation for
Rosmarie Waldrop. *Harper's* poet. Who uses
periods for rests, transitions, surprises. And Hannah
Höch, collage artist, Dada period. Pre WWII.
In confrontation of similarities. Then and now.
Of unease. Then and now. Of despair.
And in memory of Tom Blackstone. 1947-2016.
Mentally challenged. Artist. His collage on meat
hangs in our house. Where the people who lived here
before were 85% meat. Not silicon. Not even a mix.

1.
Would our predecessors be happy? With what we've done?
Our care of the yard? How we filled in the low spots.
Added patios & walkways. Stones & stories.
Astilbe & Missouri primrose. The last now blooming
a perfect yellow. The way we've cared for and loved
these walls? Which house our hopes. Passions. Our
endless search. For connection & meaning.

2.
I know. Some of the people who lived here. When
the house was still small & the empty space around
it large. One told me. They'd planted many trees.
In the backyard. The huge blue spruce just a baby
when she left. A swing (gone now) hung from one
of those trees. She liked the greenhouse we added.
We've made mistakes. All of us. The meat collage
wasn't Tom Blackstone's either. I didn't know.

3.
It is quiet here. This early summer Sunday. Front yard.
Just sun & shade. Me rocking ever so mildly
on a chair. We reclaimed from the trash. Slight breeze.

Fresh air. A few cars. Now and then. Across the street.
Jack (knees bone on bone) backs down his drive.
The scooter he needs dangles from his trailer like a kid's
bike. He stops at the crossroads. A complete stop. Like
an end. Then disappears around the corner. Two days ago

4.
Jack drove across our street. Rode his scooter
into our house. Where the people who lived here
before still linger. He joined us for chicken
on leaf lettuce I picked from the back garden.
The people who lived here before approved.
Jack is 94 and misses Marty. Who died right
before Christmas. I miss her, too. All of them

5.
really. Mother. Who spent her last few years near
here. Wished she could go back to the farm. One
more time. My sis. Who tried so hard. To keep
the family together. My brother's wife. After cancer
ravaged everything. Except her soul. Friends. Old
times. Wild buttercups in the back field. Of my youth.
I miss all the people who lived here before. The ones
I knew. The ones I didn't. The predecessors. Those
yet to be.

6.
I miss you, too, my Love. Gone to a party I skipped.

7.
Stuart. Young, unmarried. Built the house next door.
In the empty lot the people who lived here before owned.
Just drove his black 4X4 into his brand new double
garage. He left half an hour ago. And already is back.
Will he water his newly planted Buffalo grass next?

Will he find a wife? Bring her home to live? Grow
children to play on the Buffalo grass?
Steve. Two houses south on Jack's side of the street.
Walks his dog (almost pony-sized) past our house.
He waves. At an oncoming car. Doesn't see me.
Sitting so still in my reclaimed chair.

8.
The flag by our sidewalk. (Set among mini-boulders
my daughter brought from Kansas. For our new house.)
Also waves. In the gentle air. So peaceful this place.
Where the people before us lived. I wonder, Love

9.
will you be home soon? It's nice here. Pre WWIII.
Where people have lived before. But it's better when
you are sitting in the chair beside me. Also reclaimed
from the trash. Which matches mine. Just so.

endless search

The Pictures Are Back on the Walls

and fresh red roses
wrapped in pink tissue
greet curious visitors
armed with well-wishes.

We begin again, you
and I, putting old belongings
in new context,
and our disagreements, too,

seem less steep, more
manageable, like the flat
drive and the main-floor
laundry and the bedroom

with zero steps leading to it.
Even the taxes are half
what they were on the one
that served us fine

for decades before retirement,
an angry economy,
and increasingly hard words
demanded change. Risk

is an extra-high bed set in
a correct Feng Shui direction
and a gentle attitude hung
above the double-sink mirror.

Our old white curtains
sway softly
over an unexpectedly
gorgeous view.

                              begin again

Lady Jekyll's Story

Ever sweet, gracious, refined
and nice, each day
Lady greeted her home-coming
husband with praise, smiles, a slice
of chocolate cake still warm.

For years she never even saw Mr. Hyde

but one day she ran out of chocolate
and discovered him frowning
from the chair where the Doctor always sat.
She covered her surprise with her harm-
less tongue, where it rested unchallenged.

A few days later she added more surprise.

Then more. In time she learned she could
sorcerer Mr. Hyde with a few simple code
words (a difficult family member's name,
certain financial terms) or even just a tone
(disdain, criticism, chastisement).

The surprise grew hard and so sticky

her tongue stuck to the roof of her mouth,
turning nice into something the texture of ice.
That was when she first met Mrs. Hyde.
Her surprise was so great it exploded
with a fury of recrimination, then regret,

then penance. After the ashes settled,
she shooed Mr. Hyde
out of the garden
with a rag of knowledge.
When the Doctor returned, frail
and hale, they laughed and laughed

then took a walk, holding hands.

sorcerer

Snow Crab Apple Tree

Every morning a blue jay
flies into the snow crab tree
outside my kitchen window

scolds and scolds
the baby owl nesting there
who, to all appearances,

never seems to notice.
I know a woman like that
at my church, and the church

just shuts its eyes, waiting
for the woman to be done.
All the neighborhood children

like to come over, watch
the blue jay scold the owl. Every
spring the tree blooms, too.

                                                    re-blooms

Lion: ace, adventurer, aggressive, big cheese, big deal, big gun, big name, big shot, big stuff, bigwig, brave, celeb, celebrity, champion, conqueror, cynosure, daredevil, demanding attention, demigod, dignitary, diva, exemplar, fearless, gallant, god, goddess, great person, heavy, famous person, fearless, fierce, figure, heavyweight, hero, heroine, hotshot, ideal, idol, immortal, lead, leader, luminary, magnate, mahatma, major leaguer, masterful, model, notable, protect, purest grade, rage, roar, royal, somebody, someone, spirited, star, strong, superstar, the cheese, unafraid, unignorable, VIP, vicious, victor, worthy.

How You Know I'm Mad: A Response to Your Poem in 7 Parts
For my much-loved spouse, who doesn't like angry women.

1. She leaves the party and walks around.
Yes. Fumes radiate from my body. If
I don't get out, I'll explode and embarrass us
both. Leaving is a better alternative.
You don't really listen anyway.

2. She walks home.
Not if it's too far, too hot, too cold
or dangerous. I'm mad, not dumb. Though,
in the other sense, I might as well be
since you have no interest in what I might say.

3. The silent treatment.
You silence me. You ask: Why
do you always personalize everything?
Your voice grows even though we're public.
You start to swear, catch yourself. We're public.
Besides, I tried to tell you. You didn't listen.

4. She sleeps alone.
a. It's a protest. It's a feeble protest,
but a protest nonetheless. b. I am still racing inside
and would only toss and turn. c. I don't much
like you right now. d. I'd talk it out, but you'd
just complain about my waking you up
in the middle of the night to talk. e. All of the above.

5. She goes to a friend's place.
a. The friend listens. b. You used
to be the friend. c. The friend understands.
d. The friend is never passive aggressive: there
will be no repercussions, no tiny punishments
from my friend for what I say. e. All of the above.

6. She won't eat my chocolate.
This is a hard one. I love your chocolate.
Hate saying no to your chocolate. Are you listening?
This is important. I almost NEVER say no
to your chocolate. ARE YOU LISTENING?

7. She scowls.
What else can I do? I'm in a trap. You control
when we talk, when we don't, what we talk about.
So far, I control my own facial expressions.

So, yes, I'm mad. I've a long litany of things
I wish you'd do that you don't do, won't do,
aren't interested in doing. I'll spare you.
I don't believe you'd listen anyway. After all,

you don't really want to hear this list, do you?
Wouldn't you prefer that I leave the party,
walk home, use the silent treatment, sleep alone,
go to a friend's, scowl?

I'm not so sure about the chocolate.

rage

I Am the Plumber's Wife

The plumber knows a lot—
who is sick, who is sleeping
with whom, who plays
with weird stuff—
but the plumber doesn't know
everything. When I went
to my urologist she said
you haven't had sex
for a long while, have you.
I don't know which was worse,
the flushing shame of being
found out or the tears of loss
I immediately plugged up.

                                              roar

On the Eve of a Hard Seventy

I woke with the vision of turning blue,
not some septic faded holey denim,
the kind I wore as a teen and lived long
enough to watch the style disappear
then return recently to racks of clothes
in quality stores with senseless price tags

nor the pale sky-blue of a bright summer
day, just the way it was on the late August
date when I turned seventy, a blue
that shouted light-hearted joy completely foreign
to the actual event

which started out with an email
from my old high school buddy Mary, the one
who moved to Mexico when she married
and four decades later we reconnected
via cyberspace and she wished me
*a memorable 70th birthday and that the coming
year brings you only success and joy*

and then confided that her beloved cancer-
wracked spouse had finally succumbed early
Saturday morning and added a long missive
detailing the scene, how they had foregone
a religious service as he wanted, but had turned
out to have one anyway, the family—all dressed
in Yucatan beige and white (*guayaberas*) gathering
around him, sharing memories and tears and more,
and how they had *left the coffin open so everyone
could say a Last good bye, except for one grandson
who just couldn't bear the idea of seeing his "Abu"
gone,* no it wasn't that kind of sky-blue at all

but rather, it was a cobalt blue I was turning, my skin
just suddenly becoming that startling, rich, unignorable
blue that so often crams the pages of today's most
sophisticated decorator magazines, skin so
shocking that it stuck out, demanding attention,
not denial, and after that it didn't bother
me to be turning seventy since this new
brilliant blue somehow made me beautiful.

            cynosure

The Mail Arrives Late

here in our new house
but I am not complaining
because the one I love best
still sleeps beside me every night
still tells me I'm the best looking
woman around still reaches
for my hand at the movies still
wants to show me the old farm
where one of his cousins once
beat him up in an era where cousins
were bullies and you had to lie
to survive

but here in our new house
the one I love best
need never lie again
because I am strong
here in our new house

and I will protect him
from the bullies of his long-ago
youth who didn't even recognize
an angel when they saw one, let alone
realize that if you hurt an angel
he will forgive you over and over.

                                                        protect

Things My Husband Doesn't Know I Do

How I hurry to fold the bedspread
every night before he does because
otherwise next morning it takes me forever
to figure out which way to lay the cloth.

How I curse inside when I discover
he put the utensil rack in the dishwasher
just the way he likes it when I've told him
over and over the way I like it.

How I grumble when he lays his keys,
wallet, pocket change and little red
notebook on the kitchen counter
I just finally got all cleaned off.

How I know these things I do that he
doesn't know I do are petty and not
pretty and how if he were to die I'd miss
all these stupid meaningless things

even more than the amazing list of wonders
he does that he doesn't think I acknowledge
with proper gratitude, attitude, latitude
but I do, I do, he just doesn't know.

worthy

Haven

All around us people
are leaving for heaven,
that place in your mind
where Mother still pets
our cats and the world peace
you request when waitresses
ask what else you'd like

really emerges, and sure
it sounds lovely, like going
to the beach or a resort
where the only thing to do
is have fun.

I wish them well, but, no
I don't want to go yet,
I just want to hang out
with you amidst the clutter
we've collected and the smell
of chocolate chip cookies
baking in the kitchen
and white sheets wrinkled
with the TV remote handy
just the way you like.

                                                royalty

Another Breadstick Please
for April

For this hot, fast food
cheap and quick, served
with a kind smile
and no expectation of reciprocation

I give thanks this holy day.

For this simple red chair,
the laminated table, the paper napkins,
the bottomless fountain drink
and the pleasure of dawdling un-reproached

I give thanks this holy day.

For the spouse at home who shares
my life, opens and shuts each day
with words well-worked
into a litany of tenderness and care

I give thanks this holy day.

For the family and friends
who measure my worth
by my presence instead of my deeds
or abilities or social standing or cash

I give thanks this holy day.

For the joy I experience day after day,
hour after hour, second after second
in a world which promises less and less
freedom year after year

I give thanks this holy day.

For this moment of quiet pleasure,
of saying "another breadstick please"
and receiving two
when one would surely do

I give thanks this holy day.

                                                          spirited

May Day

Cold rain with snow predicted. Yesterday—
the last of a week of glorious sun—I planted
baby annuals. Today I rush to cover
their vulnerability with old sheets, wrap
three hanging baskets in terrycloth, close
the soft material with red plastic
clothes pins I found in this, my new
old home, the downsizing nearly complete.

I remember being a little short of seven
and filling homemade paper baskets with candy,
wild violets and John-Deere-yellow dandelions.
Mother drove me from the farm into town
where I selectively placed my precious
gifts by various doorways, ever quick to run
away before my identity was discovered.

I raised my children in seven different houses.
Nobody marked May Day this way in the first
six, but in the seventh, the one that lasted
thirty years, the doorbell rang on May 1st.
We found cups with popcorn, candy, and a few
store-bought posies by our front steps. Some
rituals don't die, they simply commute.

This is my eighth house since my first child
arrived. Now seven decades in, I sit
fearless in a tiny room I claim as my new office,
look out the window at my new old trees
scarcely swaying in the still-mild wind.
A storm promises worse tomorrow, but I am
unafraid of this coming change because over
time I've discovered that new flowers always
overflow my cup with reliability and surprise.

                                              unafraid

Sarah Voss is a retired Unitarian Universalist minister, a past math professor, a contract chaplain at Methodist Hospital in Omaha, the author of many works about religion and math/science (dedicated website: www.PiZine.org), a lucky grandmother, an incurable poet (interview: http://rkvryquarterly.com/interview-with-sarah-voss/), and a mystic (interview: http://www.centerforsacredsciences.org/index.php/Holos/holos-voss.html). She and her spouse Dan Sullivan—both young-at-heart—live in an old farmhouse in the middle of Omaha.

Sarah's poetry has appeared in such print journals as *Writer's Journal, Ellipsis, Earth's Daughters, The MidWest Quarterly* and *The Mid-America Poetry Review*; in collections including *Nebraska Presence: An Anthology of Poetry* and *Times of Sorrow, Times of Grace*; and online in *r.k.v.r.y Quarterly, Midway Journal*, and *Sacred Journey*. In 1991, while completing her hospital training as a chaplain, Sarah produced a very well-received chapbook of poem-prayers for the Department of Pastoral Care at the Immanuel Medical Center in Omaha. Now, twenty-five years later, *Possum, Beaver, Lion: Variants* is her first traditional collection of poetry. She has been refining her poetic craft for a long time!

www.ingramcontent.com/pod-product-compliance
Lightning Source LLC
LaVergne TN
LVHW041556070426
835507LV00011B/1125